YOU'VE GOT ME

IN STITCHES

Tippit

"Nasty little cough you have there."

YOU'VE GOT ME
IN STITCHES

Edited by LAWRENCE LARIAR

A new collection of the funniest cartoons of
all time about doctors, patients, and hospitals
by the nation's foremost artists

DODD, MEAD & COMPANY   NEW YORK

ISBN: 0-396-06821-9
Library of Congress Catalog Card Number: 73-3905
Printed in the United States of America

FOREWORD

When the first edition of *You've Got Me in Stitches* was published two decades ago, critics and public greeted it with hilarious huzzahs. It soon became a best seller, loaded with laughter, a manual of medical mirth.

Herewith, in this new and up-to-date edition, readers will find the freshest and funniest stock of hospital humor, a titillating compendium of tomfoolery, aimed at the funny bone of all hospitalized folk, including patients, interns, doctors, nurses, and visitors.

Anybody who thinks there isn't an important reason for a book of this type had best hurry to the nearest hospital for proof. A recent survey of hospitalized patients, taken by the Hospitalized Patients Survey Company, shows a remarkable lack of things to do while waiting for the incisions to heal. A poll of 3,876 patients revealed the following breakdown of their leisure:

1,345 patients admitted they spent all their waking hours gazing vacantly at the ceiling;

856 confessed they stared out the window looking for birds, planes, blimps, clouds, flying saucers, or any other airborne objects;

3,091 (males) admitted they concentrated their full energies wishing for that pretty blonde nurse to come back and administer an alcohol rub.

Thirty patients had nothing to say at all, mostly because they were either (a) in a coma, (b) in the contagious-disease wing and could not be interviewed, or (c) not yet out of the ether.

The fact remains that most sick people in hospitals require strong doses of laughter and good cheer. Too often, the ordinary patient is subjected to the ultimate in mental cruelty while waiting for the happy day when he will be dismissed. As soon as the operation proves a success or the disease shows signs of being defeated, the unfortunate convalescent finds himself facing the greatest ordeal of all—the steady flow of well-wishers who come to torment him during visiting hours.

These purveyors of joy and gladness should be carefully screened by a trained psychologist before being allowed to enter any sickroom. Such an analysis might go a long way toward shortening the convalescent period of the patient, since not a few of the guests seem to affect the patient in a negative way, causing sudden loss of breath, bubbling blood pressure, migraine headaches, spots before the eyes, heaves, and hot and cold running depressions.

A lack of space allows only a quick breakdown of the various types of lunatic allowed to enter a hospital room ungagged. Anybody who ever survived their tortures should recognize them at once.

1. *The Cheerful Ghoul* (or *Mournful Moaner*) who tells you about several of his friends who passed into the limbo after exactly the same type of operation you had.

2. *The Silent Sympathizer* (or *Dumb Dunderhead*) who has nothing at all to say, but sits staring at you misty-eyed.

3. *The Noisy Comic* (or *Happy Hooligan*) who lets fly with a barrage of loud jokes, quips, and anecdotes he'd never dare tell you if you had your strength and were able to hit him.

4. *The Hungry Hound* (or *Apple Stealer*) who has dropped by only because he wants to ravage your gift candy, fruits, and nuts.

5. *The Family Fusspot* (or *Chum Collector*) who has scrupulously combed the country to bring you a cozy covey of relatives you haven't seen for decades and had hoped to avoid for the rest of your life.

This book was conceived as an antidote to all the above well-intentioned charmers. It was created to bring your sick friend the ultimate in enjoyment. The intelligent and thoughtful visitor need only follow a few simple rules to qualify as a welcome guest in any hospital in the land.

Simply go to your nearest bookstore and purchase this book. Next, lay the volume gently within reach of your sick friend. And finally, go home.

Lawrence Lariar

Freeport, N.Y.

Gerard

"This is Mr. Gillespie. He's the gentleman who wrote that highly controversial book entitled 'The Hospital-Doctor Racket.'"

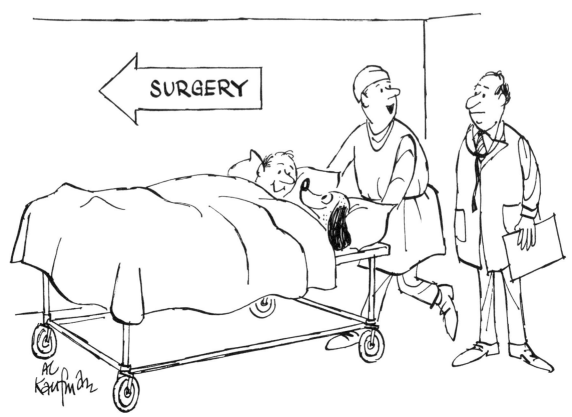

SURGERY

Kaufman

"They're inseparable!"

Lariar

". . . and you always tell the patient it was the worst-looking
appendix you ever took out!"

Fox

"I'll have you out of here in a week—one way or the other."

Day

"One every two hours—
and it's _a_ pill, not _the_ pill."

Johns

"Let me put it this way . . . if you were a building
you'd be condemned."

"You're fine, thanks, Doctor. How am I?"

Ketcham

Isler

Tippit

*"Well, it's not exactly the diagnosis I had in mind,
but I guess it'll have to do."*

Garel

"Bill, go downstairs to the phone booth, call this place, ask how I'm doing, and come back and tell me, will ya?"

Willoughby

"Admit it—you medical people haven't devised a decent new sickness for years!"

Orehek

"I hope you don't mind, Father . . . I'm going to give you a miracle drug!"

3

2

1

Tippit

Willoughby

"That's quite a suture!"

Wilkinson

"I'd say offhand he has a fever!"

Cramer

Kaufman

"Are you sure you're taking that vitamin prescription?"

Keate

*"I suppose this washes me up as president of the
local Planned Parenthood League . . ."*

Lepper

*"It's Dr. Brown calling to see if you feel better at 3 A.M. today
than when you called him at 3 A.M. yesterday."*

Marcus

"NURSE!"

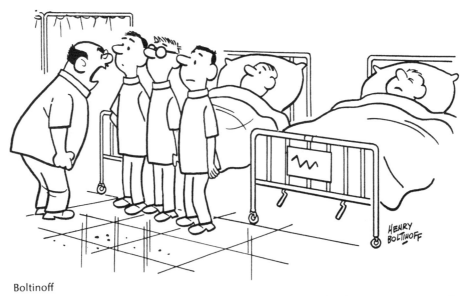

Boltinoff

"We don't have pools here on whose patient has the highest temperature!"

Lepper

"I liked the way you told him what to do with the thermometer."

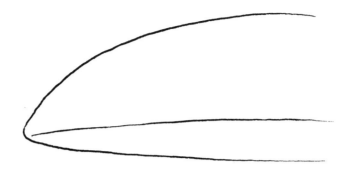

NEATNESS
COUNTS

Day

"Hello, children, goodbye, outboard motor."

Zib

"My diagnosis shows that your blood pressure is back to normal, but you still have a bad slice in your putt."

Orehek

*"I hope I'm not getting too personal,
but could you tell me how I am?"*

Dole

"The accident-prone patient is here, Doctor."

Day

*"Those TV shows have taught me one thing—
the surlier you are, the more they respect you."*

Dole

"Then I told her she had no supernatural powers at all."

Levine

"Mrs. Lanson wants to know about the one pink pill before
breakfast, two yellow after each meal and one blue at bedtime—
she's color blind."

Bo Brown

Day

chon
Day

*"Now about the obstetrical fee—
do we pay you or the taxi driver?"*

Willoughby

"First, let's discuss how sick you can afford to be!"

1

2

3

Lepper

Mirachi

"Hear anything expensive?"

Garel

"Do you think a lousy lollipop will make up for what you did to me?"

"But I'm not equipped to feed triplets!"

Willoughby

Salkin

"Chill."

"I don't care what she insisted
—that girdle comes off!"

Zib

Day

"We prefer calling it an 'inoculation' rather than a 'fix.'"

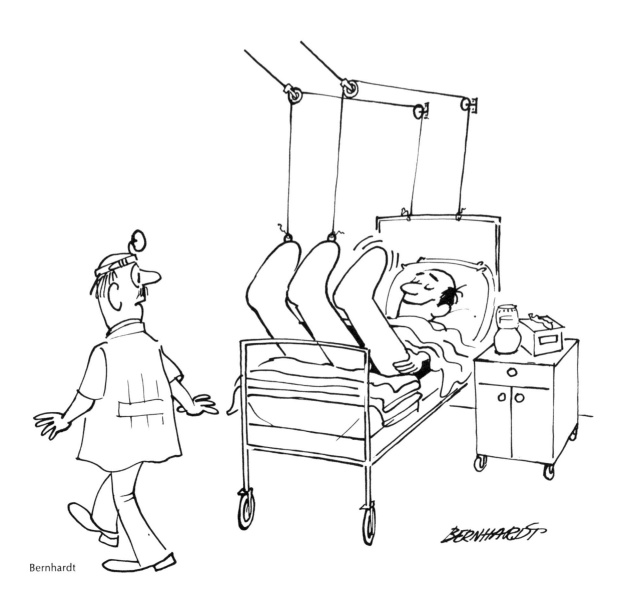

Bernhardt

Keller

"Your pot runneth over."

Pearson

"*Miss Locke, I wish you wouldn't refer to hypodermic injections as your needlework.*"

Schochet

"Give him two aspirin and rush him to the hospital."

Orehek

"Take this prescription to any barbershop!"

Polston

"Stay inside more and get some fresh air."

Brown

"Want me to take a stab at it?"

Dole

Zib

"Let me simplify it for you, Doc. Picture an artery loaded with cholesterol . . ."

Wilkinson

Zib

"I'm sorry, Mrs. Clayborne—I cannot accept
a Chinese fortune cookie as a second opinion!"

"Mind if I look around?
I was born here."

Ross

O'Brien

"Congratulations—it's a baby!"

Isler

Zib

"Hello—Dr. David Reuben . . . ?"

Gerard

"Wine and women are out, but you can sing in moderation!"

"Medical schools aren't producing enough doctors—I guess we'll have to marry businessmen."

Bo Brown

Zib

"... because I'm about to venture into the great, pure outdoors—that's why I'm not removing it!"

GALLAGHER

Gallagher

"Let me tell you, you were

a very sick basketball player!"

Lariar

"The scissors are missing . . . pass the word along!"

Roth

"You have tonsilitis complicated by that $109
you've owed me for two years!"

Drummond

Lepper

"... *The hip bone's connected to the thigh bone,*
the thigh bone's connected to the knee bone,
the knee bone's connected to the leg bone ..."

Willoughby

"Is this your first time?"

Tippit

"That's a lot more allowance than I give my kids."

"It needs a rest."

Day

Bo Brown

"Now, Reverend, turn the other cheek, please."

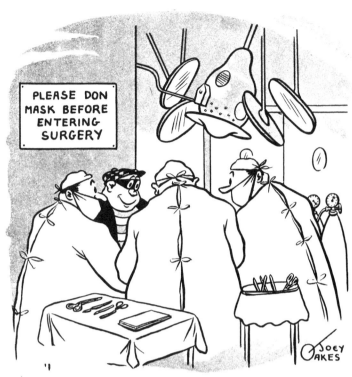

Oakes

Orehek

"It hurts when I run!"

Zib

"You have a forked tongue, Chief."

FILCHOCK

Filchock

"Don't say anything that would cause her to change her mind!"

Dennis

"Mom's pregnant."

Dole

Kaufman

Wilkinson

"All that I know is that the ticket broker said they were front row seats to an opening!"

Zib

"I'm a *medical* *doctor*, not a 'dirty old man'—now disrobe!"

Isler

Orehek

"You're in luck . . . I worked my way through med school as a TV repairman."

Willoughby

*"Ordinarily I don't handle cases out of my office, but
if you'd care to remove your clothes, I'll have a look at you."*

Gerard

"You mean you want an appointment THIS YEAR?"

Day

"Get straight to bed with a bottle of whiskey."

1

CONT

2

CONTAGIOUS
WARD

m. leung

Leung

Day

"*Very well, sulk!*"

O'Neal

"Hurt?"

". . . and divide by two!"

"Cut Private Tucker's vitamins 50 percent, Miss Parks!"

Quinn

*"Imagine! Telling me I'm in perfect health.
How does a quack like that stay in business?"*

Corka

"What do I do if the stork comes while you're gone?"

Boltinoff

"Just makeup. This is being televised."

Kaz

"Good heavens! He got out of the wrong side of the bed this morning!"

Orehek

"I prescribe the same treatment to anyone asking for free medical advice at a party."

Ericson

"Take one upon going to bed, and the other if you
wake up in the morning."

Boltinoff

"The doctor refused to come to the house,
but he sent a nice get-well card."

Orehek

"Congratulations! You liberated a 7-pound, 3-ounce,
brand-new feminist!"

Bo Brown

"Here's a get-well card from the hospital—they need the room."

"I hate to wake him—he had a rather restless night."

Price

"Pulse, 80; temperature, 103; income, 25,000 net."

Ross

Kaufman

"And that's the first dollar I borrowed to get through medical school."

Corka

Goldstein

"Yours is a common enough personality problem, Mr. Rankley—
you're obnoxious."

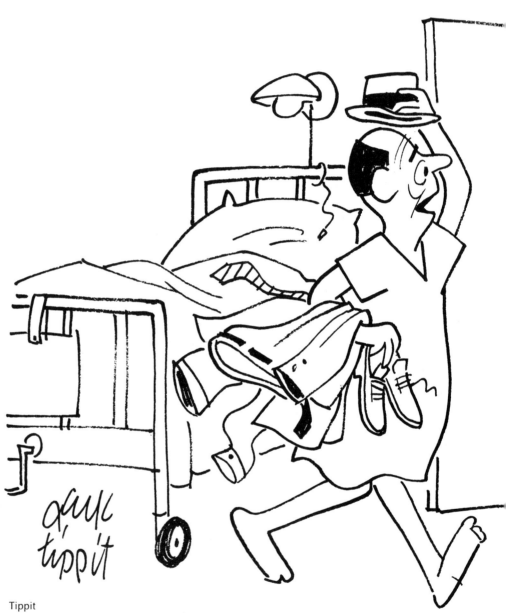

Tippit

"Did someone say <u>surgery</u>?"

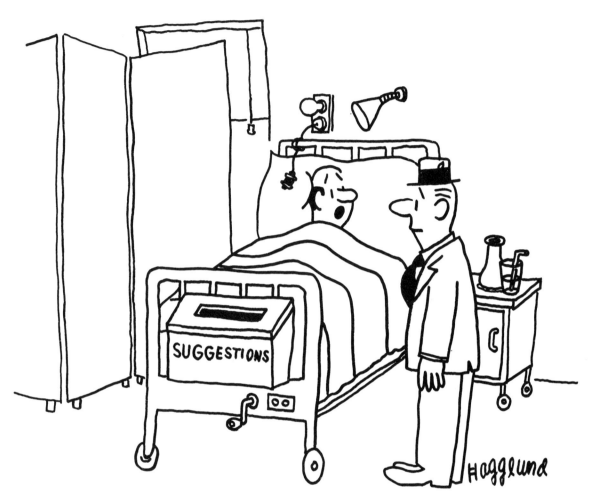

Hagglund

"They can't figure out my case!"

Marcus

*"Would you mind going to the medical convention
with me this week, all expenses paid?"*

Syverson

"Gad! I wish you could see this!"

1

MATERNITY
DELIVERY
ROOM

2

MATERNITY
DELIVERY
ROOM

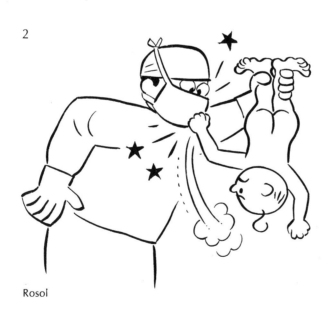

Rosol

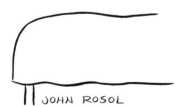

JOHN ROSOL

Sharp

"I've discovered a cure for which there is no known disease!"

Scott Brown

"General Hospital, but don't worry—I'm just going to visit a sick friend."

Zib

"Don't ask me. I'm just here taking notes for my next best seller."

Bernhardt

"Just inhale—no need to pant."

Bernhardt

"There's really nothing unusual about your condition, Mr. Phlinch, except for the fact that it is so seldom encountered in a person who is still living."

"... and no more meals. You're getting enough between meals!"

Roir

Williams

"Sorry, but I'm the only one on duty today."

Arno

ED ARNO

"I'm sorry, but under the terms of your group policy,
you don't collect unless the _entire_ group is sick."

Locke

"It's a father! I'm a girl! I'm a girl!"

*"I've found your operation very interesting,
but I'm afraid you have the wrong number."*

Day

Gerard

*"In the language of the birds and bees Miss Dunlap—
you've been pollinated!"*

Bo Brown

"Does Doctor Rafferty give stamps?"

Boltinoff

*"Has the senator been kissing babies lately?
He has chicken pox."*

"Those masks don't fool me one bit . . . I know who you are!"

Orehek

Norment

"It's me again!"

Tippit

"It sounds like fun. I must get up there some weekend and try it."

ACKNOWLEDGMENTS

The editor wishes to thank the following cartoonists for their help in gathering the funniest medical cartoons for this volume:

Arno, Bernhardt, Boltinoff, Bo Brown, Scott Brown, Corka, Cramer, Day, Dennis, Dole, Drummond, Ericson, Filchock, Fox, Gallagher, Garel, Gerard, Goldstein, Hagglund, Isler, Johns, Kaufman, Kaz, Keate, Keller, Ketcham, Lepper, Leung, Levine, Locke, Marcus, Mirachi, Norment, Oakes, O'Brien, O'Neal, Orehek, Pearson, Polston, Price, Quinn, Roir, Rosol, Ross, Roth, Salkin, Schochet, Sharp, Syverson, Tippit, Wilkinson, Williams, Willoughby, Zeis, Zib.

Thanks to the following periodicals for permission to reprint: *The American, Argosy, Better Homes and Gardens, Collier's, D A C News, Good Housekeeping, Liberty, Look, Medical Economics, Medical Tribune, Medical World News, Modern Medicine, National Enquirer, News and Notes, Official Detective, 1000 Jokes, Parade, The Physician, P.M., Saturday Evening Post, Saturday Review, Star Weekly, Today's Health, True, Wall Street Journal, Weight Watcher's Magazine.*